Baby Dinosaurs

Brachiosaurus *with its babies. It is possible that dinosaurs took care of their young after they hatched.*

DINOSAUR BOOKSHELF

Baby Dinosaurs

Text by Peter Dodson
and
Peter Lerangis

Illustrations by Alex Nino

A Byron Preiss Book

SCHOLASTIC INC.

New York   Toronto   London   Auckland   Sydney

ISBN 0-590-40276-5

Peter Dodson was involved in preparing the text but not the illustrations for *Baby Dinosaurs*.
Cover copyright © Douglas Henderson
Cover and book design by Elizabeth Wen

12 11 10 9 8 7 6 5 4 3 2 1   0 1 2 3 4 5/9

Printed in the U.S.A.   28

First Scholastic printing, May 1990

Contents

Chapter 1

DIGGING UP THE PAST

Say the word *dinosaur* now, and everyone will know what you're talking about. But that wasn't always so. Until the beginning of the 1800's, no one had ever heard of dinosaurs. When dinosaur bones were found in an excavation site in England by William Buckland in 1818, people thought they belonged to a giant elephant.

A French scientist named Georges Cuvier tried to match the bones to an elephant's bones. Then he tried a rhinoceros's bones. In fact, he compared them to any large animal he could think of, but none of the bones matched! Cuvier proposed that the bones belonged to an extinct animal.

This was a shocking statement. At that time, people didn't know that some kinds of animals had died out forever. But because Cuvier was well-respected, other scientists believed he might be right. Both European and American scientists began searching for bones, sometimes digging with shovels and picks. They found hundreds of ancient bones that had turned to stone. These stone bones are called *fossils*.

A new science was born. It was called *paleontology*, or "the study of fossils." Before long, people accepted the idea of these ancient, extinct creatures. In 1841 a British scientist named Richard Owen named them *dinosaurs*.

How did these bones get underground? And why did they turn to stone? To understand the answers to these questions, we must look into the distant past.

TIMELINE

Million years B.C.

	1.8 Quaternary	Age of man	present- 1.8 million years
	65 Tertiary	Hoofed animals and apes appear	1.8–65
MESOZOIC ERA: **AGE OF THE DINOSAURS**	144 Cretaceous	First flowering plants Last dinosaurs	65–144
	213 Jurassic	Middle dinosaurs	144–213
	248 Triassic	First dinosaurs First mammals	213–248
	286 Permian		248–286
	360 Carboniferous		286–360
	408 Devonian	First amphibians	360–408
	438 Silurian	First land plants	408–438
	505 Ordovician		438–505
	590 Cambrian		505–590
	4.6 billion Pre-Cambrian	Early life on earth	590 million–4.6 billion years

Remember: for prehistoric times, the higher the number, the farther back in time! For example, 200 million B.C. is longer ago than 65 million B.C.

How Fossils Were Formed

The time dinosaurs lived is divided into three parts. The earliest is the *Triassic* period, the middle is the *Jurassic* period, and the last is the *Cretaceous* period. There were no people on earth at this time.

The world looked very different during the dinosaur age. Much of the world's land was covered at times by shallow seas. Water covered the land in the middle of the North American continent, including what is now Montana, Wyoming, and Colorado.

Some dinosaurs lived near rivers or lakes close to the sea. When they died, their bodies sometimes were buried in sands of the river or mud spread by the floods. The land sank beneath the sea, and more sand and mud covered the bones. After millions of years, the bones were buried several thousand feet beneath the sea. The sand and mud had turned to stone, and the bone was replaced by hard mineral — the bones had now become fossils. Finally, the rocks were pushed up out of the earth by forces that created

Earth During the Triassic

Earth During the Jurassic

Earth During the Cretaceous

mountain ranges like the Rocky Mountains and drained away the seas. Wind and rain wore down the soil and rock. And little by little, some of the bones began to stick up out of the ground, ready for a paleontologist to discover.

Whenever paleontologists see fossils sticking out of the ground, they start digging. They know there may be more underneath. Many *bone beds,* full of dinosaur skeletons, have been found this way.

After the first dinosaurs were found, paleontologists were so busy looking for large dinosaurs and spectacular skeletons that they paid little attention to smaller specimens. All that changed when a surprise discovery was made in 1923. Not only were small skeletons found — but so were dinosaur eggshells!

Chapter 2

FINDING THE FIRST EGGS

In 1923 the American Museum of Natural History in New York City sent a group of paleontologists to explore the Gobi Desert in Outer Mongolia. The year before, the group had discovered the skull of a dinosaur no one had seen before. It looked a little like a *Triceratops* skull. *Triceratops* was a dinosaur with horns on its face, like a rhinoceros. But this new skull had only low bumps on its nose. It was also much smaller than the skull of a *Triceratops*. The paleontologists realized that this dinosaur was an ancestor of *Tricer-*

atops. They gave it the name *Protoceratops*, which means "first horned face."

The museum thought the discovery was very important. They wanted the group to bring back more *Protoceratops* bones. But the group did even better than that. They found fossil eggs.

The paleontologists discovered that the eggs were four to eight inches long and two to three inches wide. Some of them were small enough to hold in your hand. They were laid together in a circle, perhaps in a hole dug in sand. A nest may have held 30 or 35 eggs. In one nest, five eggs were laid deep in the center. Eleven eggs formed a circle at a higher level. And still more eggs were laid at the next level up. For some reason, these eggs were never hatched. Inside some of the eggs were tiny *Protoceratops* skeletons.

The Growth of a Dinosaur

In 1975 two Polish paleontologists found a skull from a newly hatched *Protoceratops*.

It was two-and-a-half inches long, about as long as your middle finger.

There are *Protoceratops* skulls of all sizes in the American Museum of Natural History. One of them is small enough to fit into your palm. Its eyes were huge, compared to the size of its face. It had a pointy beak and a thin, bony plate sticking out behind its skull. This skull belonged to a baby.

From the museum's collection of skulls, we have a good idea of what *Protoceratops* looked like, and how it grew. It was about nine inches long when born, and grew to an adult length of six feet. At birth it probably weighed six ounces, about the weight of a big hamburger. But when it was fully grown, it weighed 400 pounds. That's a thousand times more than it weighed at hatching!

Its face kept changing as it grew older. On the medium-size skulls, the eyes weren't as big in relation to the rest of the face. A slight arch also started to form over the nose.

When *Protoceratops* became an adult, its skull was over two feet long. That's longer than your arm! The males looked different

A baby Protoceratops *hatching*. Protocera-tops *lived in Mongolia during the late* Cretaceous.

than the females. They had definite arches over their noses and broad, bony plates sticking out of the back of their heads. The females had less of an arch. Their bony plates were lower and not as wide.

The males probably fought among themselves. They butted heads with their thick noses. Their plates may have been brightly colored. Then they could show them off to female *Protoceratops!* It's possible that the males held their plates high and strutted before the females, like modern peacocks.

Did All Dinosaurs Hatch from Eggs?

It's hard to tell exactly how dinosaurs reproduced. There aren't very many fossils of eggshells. So paleontologists sometimes compare dinosaurs to animals of today.

What modern animals lay eggs? Chickens do, of course. First they lay eggs in a nest. Then they sit on them to keep them warm. They keep sitting on the eggs until they hatch. If the chickens didn't keep their eggs warm, the unborn babies would die.

Does that mean dinosaurs were birds, like chickens? Or were they reptiles, like lizards and snakes? Most reptiles lay eggs, too. But these reptiles don't stay with the eggs and sit on them, like chickens. They just leave them. So why don't these unborn babies die? The reptiles make sure they lay their eggs in a mound of leaves and grass or bury them in warm sand to keep them warm.

Other reptiles don't lay eggs. Some lizards and snakes keep the eggs *inside* their bodies. Their eggs are kept warm by the mother's body heat. The babies are born alive.

We think that all dinosaurs were hatched from eggs. But it's possible that some of them were carried inside their mothers, and born alive like some modern reptiles. No one knows for sure.

What Can Dinosaur Eggs Tell Us?

Think about what's inside an egg. First of all, there's the baby in the egg, called the *embryo*. Then there has to be a food supply, called the *yolk*. There's also water to prevent the embryo from drying out. There's a sac to store the body wastes in. And there's oxygen, for the embryo to breathe.

Oxygen is in the air all around us. It gets into the egg through tiny holes in the eggshell called *pores*. If you look very closely at a hen's egg, you may even see the pores. There are just enough pores to let in oxygen. If there were more, too much water vapor might leak out of the egg. Then the egg would dry out, and the embryo would die.

Paleontologists looked closely at dinosaur eggs. They found that their eggs *did* have a lot more pores than chicken eggs have. In fact, it looked as if there were too many pores. They wondered why the eggs didn't just dry out.

Paleontologists had to figure out how these embryos stayed alive. They realized the dinosaur mothers must have buried their eggs in the ground or in a mound of plants. This way the soil or plants would keep the water vapor from escaping from the egg. And all those extra pores would keep oxygen coming in.

How big were newly hatched dinosaurs? We can try to find out by comparing them to modern reptiles. Inside reptile eggs, the embryos are curled up. When they hatch, their bodies uncurl. Hatchling reptiles are two or three times longer than their eggs. Dinosaur embryos may have curled up the same way. Probably hatchling dinosaurs were also longer than their eggs.

The largest dinosaur eggs ever found were ones laid by *Hypselosaurus*. *Hypselosaurus* was a dinosaur related to the *Brontosaurus*. It was 40 to 50 feet long, about as long as three cars. But its eggs were only about nine inches long — about the size of a hubcap! A hatchling may have uncurled itself to become 18 to 27 inches long. That's about the same size as a newborn human being. And human newborns are actually *heavier*. They are seven or eight pounds, and *Hypselosaurus* babies were only three or four pounds. That's because a lot of *Hypselosaurus*'s length was in its tail. And its tail was lighter than the rest of its body.

Some dinosaur eggs are much smaller.

They held hatchlings only six to nine inches long. Those babies would have been small enough to fit in the hand of a grown woman!

We do not know how large the eggs of the largest dinosaurs were. Maybe they weren't much larger than the *Hypselosaurus* eggs. Eggs wouldn't survive if they got much bigger than that. Larger eggs have thicker shells. And thick shells are more difficult for the baby to break. If the egg was too big, the poor baby would be trapped inside!

Where Are Dinosaur Eggs Found?

Dinosaur eggs have been found in only a few places. Those places have to be rather dry. Eggs that were laid in wet, swampy areas never became fossils because eggshells don't last very long in certain kinds of water. They come apart, or *dissolve.*

For instance, the eggs of an alligator nesting in the Everglades will never fossilize. But the eggs of an ostrich on a dry African plain may have a better chance.

Brachiosaurus *protects its eggs in their nest.*
Brachiosaurus *was a huge dinosaur that lived
in Colorado, Algeria, and Tanzania during
the late Jurassic.*

In the United States, dinosaur eggs have been found in Utah and Montana. They've also been discovered in China, India, the Soviet Union, France, East Africa, Canada, and Argentina.

Many baby dinosaur bones are found near certain egg sites. But eggs or baby bones are rarely found mixed with the bones of adult dinosaurs. It seems that the babies stayed on dry land while the adults traveled to the lower swampy areas. Possibly the mothers laid their eggs in special areas far away from the water. They may have also raised their young in these areas.

There's another possibility. Maybe each dinosaur mother raised only one pair of off-spring in her life. That would mean there just weren't that many dinosaur babies.

Chapter 3

BABY SKELETONS

Mother and Children — Maiasaura

Many dinosaur skeletons have been found in the state of Montana. A lot of people who live there like to collect bones, even though they're not paleontologists. Sometimes they even discover bones from dinosaurs paleontologists have never seen before.

One summer day in 1978, a paleontologist named Jack Horner went with his friend Robert Makela to a rock shop in Montana. The owner of the shop showed them a cigar box full of unknown bones. The bones were carefully wrapped in cotton. When Horner unwrapped them, he was astounded. The shape of the bones wasn't unusual — but their tiny size was. He could tell the bones belonged to a type of dinosaur called a *duck-bill*. Duckbills were large plant-eating dinosaurs. Many of them were as long as a school bus. But this duckbill was so small that its entire skeleton could fit in the cigar box!

Horner and Makela found out that the bones had been discovered on a ranch near the Rocky Mountains. There they found a shallow hole in the ground about six feet across — and made the discovery of a lifetime. The bones of 15 baby duckbills were lying at the bottom. Next to them were bits of their eggshells.

Each baby in the nest was about three feet long, except for one runt. It had a deformed foot. They named the little dinosaur "Crooked Leg."

Horner and Makela noticed that the earth around the nest was red. But the nest was made of soft, green rock. This meant that there had been plants mixed with mud to form the nest.

They noticed something else — the babies' teeth were worn. Some of them were worn halfway to the bottom. The babies must have been chewing plants for several months. And after all this time, the babies were still together in their nest.

What did all this mean? Horner and Makela reasoned that the baby duckbills were being fed by their mother. That's why they were able to stay in their nest for so long. Nowadays reptile mothers don't feed their young. But bird mothers do. So these dinosaurs behaved more like birds than like reptiles! In fact, many paleontologists believe birds are descended from dinosaurs.

Horner thinks that the babies starved to death. But why? Probably because their mother died. The babies got all of their food from their mother. Nearby, Horner and Makela found the skull of an adult duckbill that they think could have been the mother.

Horner and Makela's discovery was the first evidence that any dinosaur actually fed its young. They named these duckbills *Maiasaura,* which means "good mother lizard."

Horner thought that maybe there were even more baby maiasaurs at that spot. So he gathered a team of helpers to keep digging.

At the beginning of one summer, the crew had trouble pitching their tents. Their tent pegs kept striking rocks in the ground. They dug down and found they were trying to camp on top of a dinosaur graveyard! The "rocks" were *Maiasaura* bones! More nests with babies were discovered. Each nest had babies of a different size. The smallest babies Horner found were about 14 inches long.

Some of the nests had eggs that had never hatched. These eggs were about eight inches long — as long as a grown man's hand, from the wrist to the tip of the longest finger. Why didn't these eggs hatch? Paleontologists think the eggs may have been drowned in a flood.

A *mother* Maiasaura *and her newly hatched*
young. Maiasaura *lived in Montana during*
the late Cretaceous.

Where Did Maiasaura Live? Uplands and Lowlands

Horner noticed an interesting thing about the nest site. It contained no medium-size maiasaurs. Those kinds of dinosaurs were found farther to the north and the east. And even *farther* north and east, there were practically nothing but full-grown adults. Why was this?

A look at the land where the eggs were found might reveal an answer. It is now a high area near the Rocky Mountains. That land used to be covered by a huge sea. It was surrounded by swamps. Millions of years ago, the water drained into the ocean, and the land became dry. But back in the *Maiasaura*'s time, it was still wet and swampy.

So the eggs were laid in high, dry land, and the adults were found in a low, wet area. Horner thinks that maybe the high, dry areas were safer. Maybe there were few big meat-eaters there. Then the plant-eating dinosaurs could lay their eggs where they would not be eaten. The babies could grow up safely.

When the dinosaurs were big enough, they could travel in large herds north or south to find plenty of delicious plants.

We don't know for sure if Horner is right or not. It could be that other dinosaurs laid eggs in the swampy lowlands. But we have no way of finding out. We do know that the eggshells would have dissolved in the water over time.

Horner and Makela's discoveries are among the most important ever made about baby dinosaurs. But paleontologists have only begun to study them. In 1988 Horner found more nests and babies of another kind of duckbill. And paleontologists from Alberta, Canada, made similar finds. Five years from now, we will know more about dinosaur babies than we do today.

The "Parrot Lizard"

Many baby dinosaur skeletons have been discovered over the years. One of the most famous was forgotten for a long time. It seems hard to believe that anyone could forget about a dinosaur that looked like a parrot.

Psittacosaurus means "parrot lizard." It's the name of a small dinosaur that had a beak, like a parrot. Horned dinosaurs like the *Triceratops* and *Protoceratops* also had beaks. But they lived millions of years later. Paleontologists think that *Psittacosaurus* is an ancestor of the horned dinosaurs.

Psittacosaurus was discovered in Mongolia in 1923. It was small for a dinosaur — about as long as a tall man is high, six feet long. One of the fossils found was a baby *Psittacosaurus* skull. But the scientists in 1923 weren't interested in baby dinosaurs. In fact, they put the skull of the baby into a museum drawer — and it stayed there for 57 years!

When paleontologist Walter Coombs found it in 1980, he was amazed. It was the smallest dinosaur skull ever found — barely the size of a quarter. None of the baby's other bones were found. But paleontologists have discovered that the whole dinosaur would have been 10 inches long.

And chances are that the little *Psittacosaurus* wasn't even newly hatched. It must have been alive for a while, because its teeth were worn down from eating. That means it had probably been even smaller at one time.

A baby *Psittacosaurus* was probably pretty harmless-looking. But a baby *Stegosaurus* was another story.

Stegosaurus

Stegosaurus ate only plants, not flesh. So why was this dinosaur so scary? For one thing, it had sharp plates sticking straight up out of its back. The plates looked like huge arrowheads. At the end of its tail were big, pointy spikes. It used this armor to defend itself against ferocious meat-eaters.

Stegosaurus lived in the Jurassic period. It was a four-legged dinosaur with a small brain. Some paleontologists used to think it had two brains — one in its head and one near its hips! Actually, that's not true. The

An adult Stegosaurus *and a young* Stegosaurus *eating.*

second "brain" was really a nerve center that controlled the movement of its hind legs and tail.

An adult *Stegosaurus* could grow to be 19 feet long, about as long as a small bus. It stood as high as seven feet at the hips. That means you'd have to stand on a tall ladder to look over it. Its weight was two tons, as much as a rhinoceros or hippopotamus.

The remains of two young, small stegosaurs have also been found. One was discovered in Wyoming in 1882; the other, in Utah in 1974. The one from Utah was one or two years old. Its body was only five feet long from nose to tail, and two feet high at the hips. It was about the size of a dog, and weighed only 30 or 40 pounds.

The specimen from Wyoming is larger. It was probably eight-and-a-half feet long. It was only a year older than the other young *Stegosaurus,* but it probably already weighed 150 pounds. That's about the weight of a full-grown pig.

Chapter 4

DINOSAURS GROWING UP

It's hard to tell how old a dinosaur is just by looking at its bones. Small bones could belong to a baby dinosaur, or a young dinosaur. But they could also belong to a grown-up that just happens to be small! After all, some fully grown dinosaurs were only the size of dogs and cats.

So how can we tell the difference? The best way is to try to find many different-size skeletons of the same dinosaur. If the only *Protoceratops* skeleton ever found had been tiny, a paleontologist might think that all grown-up *Protoceratops* were tiny. But if there were a small *Protoceratops,* a medium-size one, and a big one, the paleontologist would know that the small skeleton definitely belonged to a baby, the middle one to a young dinosaur, and the big one to a grown-up. This is called a *growth series*.

Coelophysis

Paleontologists like to look for growth series. When they dig, they hope to find adult skeletons together with their babies. One of the places where they have done this is at Ghost Ranch, New Mexico.

At Ghost Ranch, there are many skeletons of a small meat-eating dinosaur called *Coelophysis*. The dinosaurs must have died in some local disaster. There were big, medium, and small skeletons. The biggest were as long as a small car. The smallest were the length of a yardstick. Where were some of the small ones found? Inside the ribs of the larger ones! It seems that some dinosaurs actually ate their young!

Allosaurus from Utah

In the Jurassic period, *Allosaurus* was the greatest meat-eater that lived. A number of skeletons of this two-legged terror were found in the American West. It was a scary beast. Its huge head had sharp, gleaming teeth. Its hands had three fingers that ended in long, pointy claws. It was about 30 feet long, with its heavy tail behind it. You couldn't put it in your living room, because its *hips* would touch the ceiling!

In central Utah, the bones of about *44* allosaurs of all different sizes have been found! They must have all died together, but we don't know why. We also don't know how all their bones got so mixed up. But studies of these bones have told us a lot. We now know how big the baby and young allosaurs were.

The smallest *Allosaurus* would have been seven or eight feet long. It probably weighed about 30 or 40 pounds. That's small for an *Allosaurus,* but it's bigger than any attack dog you've ever seen! It was probably about six months old. The next largest one was about 10 or 11 feet long and weighed 100 pounds. It was about a year old.

This kind of bone collection is a paleontologist's dream. It's a true growth series. It allows us to learn much about the way a dinosaur grew, without ever meeting one!

Another smaller dinosaur has given us a good growth series to study — *Camptosaurus* — a dinosaur that *Allosaurus* probably feasted on.

Camptosaurus

About a dozen good *Camptosaurus* skeletons were found in the state of Wyoming at a great dinosaur graveyard called Como Bluff. The skeletons were three different sizes. Some of them were as small as a dog — about five feet long and less than two feet high at the hips. They weighed about 50 pounds.

Camptosaurus lived late in the Jurassic period, 150 million years ago. Back then the

Three Camptosaurus *at different stages in their lives.*

American West was covered by rivers, lakes, swamps, and floodplains. The giant, four-legged Jurassic sauropods made the ground tremble when they walked. Their long necks stretched way up into the trees so they could snap off leaves.

But *Camptosaurus* was different. Instead of walking on four legs, it walked on two. It had a short tail, not a long one, and was only about 17 feet long. That's not exactly tiny — it's the size of a very long car — but the giant sauropods stretched to 50, 70, and maybe over 100 feet long!

Adult camptosaurs were stocky. A grown-up weighed around 2,000 pounds, as much as a large bull bison. Its skull was long and low with broad teeth. The front legs were fairly short but heavy. There were blunt claws on both the hands and the feet. Possibly they used their hands for digging up plant roots or for opening tough fruits.

Understanding the *Camptosaurus* growth series wasn't easy. At first, paleontologists thought the three different-size skeletons belonged to three different species of dinosaur.

They forgot that dinosaurs had to grow up, and that baby dinosaurs and dinosaurs that were growing up should look like adults but be smaller.

In fact, there have been many other mistakes in the discovery of growth series. Sometimes several species of dinosaur have been misnamed. Fortunately, science is a process that corrects its mistakes.

Dinosaur Mix-Ups

Between 1914 and 1935, many duckbilled dinosaur skeletons were found in Alberta, Canada. They were of different sizes. The biggest ones had bony growths on top of their heads. These growths are called *crests*. They looked something like thin, flat helmets.

Two of the dinosaurs found in Alberta were named *Lambeosaurus* and *Corythosaurus*. They were each about 30 feet long. That's about the length of a school bus.

Some medium-size dinosaurs were found. They had all smaller-size crests. But a still-smaller dinosaur was found, too. It had almost no bony crest at all. Paleontologists called it *Procheneosaurus*.

At first everyone thought the small, medium-size, and large skeletons belonged to different types or species of dinosaurs. But in 1975 a discovery was made by Peter Dodson, the co-author of this book. He measured all the skulls. The *Procheneosaurus* skulls were the smallest. The largest belonged to the *Lambeosaurus* and the *Corythosaurus*. Then he measured all the ones in the middle. Dodson noticed something interesting. The smallest skulls had no bony crests at all. But as the skulls became bigger so did the crests.

It reminded Dodson of a modern bird called the *cassowary*. Baby cassowaries show no crests on their heads. Neither do half-grown ones. The crest only begins to grow when the bird is nearly a grown-up.

Dodson had realized something no one else had: These dinosaurs weren't different types after all. Most of them were the *same* dinosaurs. They were just different ages. In fact, there was really no such animal as the

From left: Young Corythosaurus *and* Lambeosaurus; *adult* Lambeosaurus *and* Corythosaurus.

Procheneosaurus. It was just a young *Cory-thosaurus* or *Lambeosaurus.*

When Is a Camptosaurus Not a Camptosaurus?

In 1970 a growth series was discovered in northern Wyoming and Montana for a type of *Camptosaurus.* At least, it was *thought* to be a *Camptosaurus.*

The series puzzled paleontologists. The fully grown dinosaurs looked rather like camptosaurs and were the same size. Like camptosaurs, they were two-legged plant-eaters with thick legs, and long tails. There were some differences, but the adult skeletons showed many similarities to the skeletons of dinosaurs that had been called camptosaurs since 1884.

But the younger dinosaurs in the growth series didn't look like young camptosaurs at all. Their legs were long and slender, like the legs of small, swift dinosaurs. As they grew up, their legs became bigger and thicker. *Camp-*

tosaurus had big, thick legs even when they were babies. These young dinosaurs weren't camptosaurs at all.

Scientists had discovered a completely different kind of dinosaur, and Yale University paleontologist John Ostrom named it *Tenontosaurus* in 1970.

There's one thing we know for sure: The two dinosaurs never met to talk about their differences — or even grunt. That's because the last *Camptosaurus* died about 150 million years ago. And the first *Tenontosaurus* didn't appear until 50 million years later!

Now we've discussed baby dinosaurs and young dinosaurs. There's also another group of small dinosaurs. These are dinosaurs that look like babies, but they're not. They're grown-up dinosaurs — very *small* grown-up dinosaurs.

Chapter 5

BABIES OR
SMALL ADULTS:
WHICH IS WHICH?

Compsognathus

The very first almost-complete dinosaur skeleton was discovered in Germany in 1861. It was a small dinosaur, which paleontologists named *Compsognathus*. No other *Compsognathus* skeleton was found for over 100 years. But in 1972 a larger one was discovered in France.

The German skeleton was about 14 inches long from the tip of its nose to the back of its hips. We can guess that its tail added another 12 inches to its length. So it was a little

The small Compsognathus *ate even smaller
lizards.* Compsognathus *lived in southern
France and Germany during the late Jurassic.*

over two feet long. That's not much longer than your arm. The French specimen was about three feet long.

Compsognathus was a meat-eater. Its head was only three inches long. But that's large compared to the rest of its body. It reminds us of another meat-eater with a huge head — the monster dinosaur of all time, *Tyranno-saurus*. In fact, *Compsognathus* was shaped like *Tyrannosaurus*. It walked on its hind legs, with a long tail and short front legs. But *Tyrannosaurus* was a giant, and *Compsog-nathus* was only the size of a rooster, weigh-ing only two or three pounds. It probably used its sharp teeth for eating insects or small lizards.

Nowadays we know of baby dinosaurs that were smaller than the skeleton of *Compsog-nathus*. But did the *Compsognathus* skeleton belong to a baby or a grown-up? It's hard to tell. It has a large head and very large eye sockets — which is what we would expect to find in a baby. But this kind of shape *could* also be found in a small-size grown-up, too.

We don't know the answer. But if *Comp-*

sognathus grew to only three feet long, it would truly be among the smallest adult dinosaurs known.

Hypsilophodon

Hypsilophodon was a plant-eater that lived 100 million years ago, in the early Cretaceous period. Large specimens of *Hypsilophodon* are only about six-and-a-half feet long. Because of the way their bodies slanted, they were probably about your size. They weighed approximately 50 pounds, as much as a small sheep or medium-size dog.

Much smaller skeletons than grown *Hypsilophodon* have been found in England. These skeletons were about three feet long and weighed less than 10 pounds. That's smaller than some well-fed cats.

Hypsilophodon had long legs, so it must have been a swift runner. At first that seems strange. After all, plant-eaters don't have to run fast to catch their food! For a while paleontologists thought *Hypsilophodon* lived in trees. They thought its legs would be good for climbing. But now we don't believe this to be true. It's a good bet that the *Hypsilophodon* needed its long legs for something else. It had to run fast to escape from quick little meat-eaters, who wanted to take a bite out of it!

The "Mouse Lizard"

Imagine a dinosaur so small that it's named after a mouse! In South America in 1976, two paleontologists found such a dinosaur.

The dinosaur was named *Mussaurus,* which means "mouse lizard." Actually, it's closer to the size of a kitten, about 10 inches long. Still, this tiny plant-eater is the smallest complete skeleton of a dinosaur ever found. Its skull was an inch-and-a-quarter long, not even as long as your pinkie. Its thighbone and shinbone were even smaller.

Mussaurus is one of the oldest dinosaurs ever found. It was discovered by a paleontologist named José Bonaparte. But Bona-

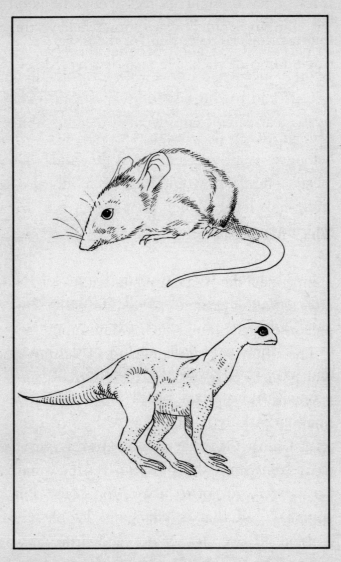

A newborn baby Mussaurus *was the size of a mouse.*

parte didn't find just one *Mussaurus*. He found *six* altogether. Four of them were in a single lump of rock. He also discovered several eggs, which were only an inch long. We're not sure that those were the eggs of *Mussaurus*. In fact, we're not even sure they belonged to a dinosaur. But if they did, that means a newborn would have been only two-and-a-half inches long. That's *truly* the size of a mouse.

In this book, we've discussed some of the very best examples of small dinosaurs and baby dinosaurs. But there are many others. In fact, there are whole groups of dinosaurs that were small, even as grown-ups.

In all, almost *half* of all dinosaurs were small. Years ago people were mostly concerned with the great giants. And as we've seen, sometimes the most interesting small fossils were forgotten about for years! But nowadays all that is changing. People are looking all over for babies and little dinosaurs. They realize that to understand the world of the great dinosaurs, sometimes it's necessary to think small.

Bagaceratops *with its young*. Bagaceratops *was a small dinosaur (three-and-a-half feet long) that lived in Mongolia during the late Cretaceous.*

Pronunciation Guide

Allosaurus   **Al**-o-**saw**-rus

Brontosaurus   **bront**-o-**saw**-rus

Camptosaurus   **camp**-to-**saw**-rus

Coelophysis   **see**-lo-**fise**-iss

Compsognathus   **comp**-sog-**nay**-thus

Corythosaurus   ko-**rith**-o-**saw**-rus

Hypselosaurus   **hip**-sel-o-**saw**-rus

Hypsilophodon   **hip**-si-**loff**-o-don

Lambeosaurus   **lam**-bee-o-**saw**-rus

Maiasaura   **my**-a-**saw**-ra

Mussaurus	muss-**aw**-rus
Protoceratops	**pro**-toe-**serr**-a-tops
Psittacosaurus	**sit**-a-ko-**saw**-rus
Stegosaurus	**steg**-o-**saw**-rus
Triceratops	try-**serr**-a-tops
Tyrannosaurus	tie-**ran**-o-**saw**-rus

ABOUT THE CONTRIBUTORS

PETER LERANGIS graduated from Harvard College with a degree in biochemistry. His more than 25 published works include *Time Machine #22: The Last of the Dinosaurs* and *Explorer #3: In Search of a Shark!*

PETER DODSON, Ph.D., is currently associate professor of animal biology and teacher of veterinary anatomy at the University of Pennsylvania School of Veterinary Medicine. Author of more than 30 scientific works, including *Evolution, Process and Product*, co-authored with his father, Edward O. Dodson, he has worked for a number of seasons in the dinosaur beds of western Canada and the United States. He is also co-editor of *The Dinosauria*, to be published in 1990 by the University of California Press.

ALEX NINO'S work has appeared in such publications as France's *Metal Hurlant* and America's *Starlog*. His paintings and illustrations have been published as portfolios, book jackets, and graphic stories. He is also the winner of the Inkpot Award.